A
CALENDAR *of*
RECKONING

Other Coteau Books by Dave Margoshes

A Book of Great Worth
Wiseman's Wager
Long Distance Calls

A

CALENDAR *of*

RECKONING

DAVE MARGOSHES

Edited by Maureen Scott Harris
Cover art: "The reckoning of Delilah" by Sarah-jane Newman, 12" x 12", oil on canvas
Printed and bound in Canada

Library and Archives Canada Cataloguing in Publication

Margoshes, Dave, author
    A calendar of reckoning / Dave Margoshes.

Poems.
Issued in print and electronic formats.
ISBN 978-1-55050-937-3 (softcover).--ISBN 978-1-55050-938-0 (PDF).--
ISBN 978-1-55050-939-7 (HTML).--ISBN 978-1-55050-940-3 (Kindle)

    I. Title.

PS8576.A647C35 2018   C811'.54   C2017-907180-7
                                            C2017-907181-5

2517 Victoria Avenue
Regina, Saskatchewan
Canada S4P 0T2
www.coteaubooks.com

Available in Canada from:
Publishers Group Canada
2440 Viking Way
Richmond, British Columbia
Canada V6V 1N2

10 9 8 7 6 5 4 3 2 1

Coteau Books gratefully acknowledges the financial support of its publishing program
by: the Saskatchewan Arts Board, The Canada Council for the Arts, the Government of
Saskatchewan through Creative Saskatchewan, the City of Regina. We further acknowl-
edge the [financial] support of the Government of Canada. Nous reconnaissons l'appui
[financier] du gouvernement du Canada.

For dee, who inspires me

And in memory of Paddy O'Rourke, my first publisher

Contents

1. An Ordinary Child: a Postmodern Autobiography

2. Topsy-Turvy

3: The Ripening

4. The Road Going On, or Feral Indirection

1

An Ordinary Child:
a Postmodern Autobiography

Birthday

I was born on a day in July, my father liked to say,
when the birds ceased their singing, held their breath,
gathered in silent flocks on the highest branches
the better to see, a day when the rickety earth seemed
to pause on its axis and even the activity of angels
in heaven came to an abrupt stop, as if to note
the occurrence of something extraordinary, my father
said. But no, I protested, I was an ordinary child,
third and last child to my loving parents, first son
with two sceptical sisters to reckon with, born on
an ordinary day in the all-too-ordinary month
of July, but, agreed, in an extraordinary year, when
there was war to contend with, war and fear
and a shifting along fault lines, but still,
an ordinary child born to an ordinary family,
the start of an ordinary life, nothing for birds
to concern themselves with, let alone angels. But
no, my father insisted, the sky held its breath that day,
pulling the air out of his own lungs. *I was there*,
he said, *I saw it.*

Pears

At the back of the farm, out of sight
of the house, a miniature pear orchard,
three trees, old and fruitful, a happy family.
In spring, my mother and I would take the long hike
through the meadow and across a small stream
to visit the eruption of pink fragrance, then begin
to count the days, my mother penciling them off
on the kitchen calendar: the fruit we knew
was growing would be ready in the heat of July.
In June, the small orbs began to form, seed turning
into flesh, my mother explained, just the way
I had grown inside her. Incomprehensible,
magic. By early July, the pears were full size,
starting to blush, sweetness reddening their cheeks,
but still too hard. Now we were coming every day,
armed with pails just in case, maybe tomorrow,
my mother said, day after day. But then one morning
the orchard was bare, leaves fluttering
like dispirited flags, a scattering of spoiled fruit
underfoot. This happened every summer:
expectation, hope, disappointment, a familiar rhythm.
Boys from town, my mother explained. She consulted
with my father but no trap could be devised, no altering
of our own schedule to anticipate their bitter thievery.
Sweetness in our sight, snatched away. We must learn
to be faster, I suggested. No, my mother said,
we must learn how to wait.

Daydreaming

I was thin as a promise and my sisters called me
Fatso. A quiet child, I was a long time learning
to read, couldn't skate, bit my nails to the quick.
At school, I listened with intent but heard
almost nothing though the doctor insisted
there was nothing wrong with my hearing.
Just daydreaming, he said, giving me a wink
and a squeeze on the knee that left a bruise for days,
a bruise I imagined getting in a fight over a girl.
Just daydreaming, yes, that was the problem,
and as I grew, the problem failed to abate. The sound
of the word itself attracted me, *daydream* – so much
nicer than *nightmare* – and the notion of it, dreaming
while awake, in broad daylight. I could daydream
at any time, under any conditions, though the best times
were in school near a window I saw myself climbing
through and at night as shadows from the traffic below
raced across the ceiling, me on a horse in hot pursuit.
Gradually, with the passage of time, the world I imagined
narrowed, and I put on weight, grew into myself.

Brooklyn, 1952

We board the bus together,
me first, so I take
the first empty seat,
there's plenty more further back
but that's the one she wanted.
Me 10, 11, innocent
as a certain lamb.
I don't even notice her
till she's pausing beside
me, glaring down, grey-haired,
grandmotherly. "Kike,"
she spits, lumbers on.

My Mother's Ring

The bee kissed my mother's finger
just above her wedding band
and it was either the ring or the finger,
my father said later, so they chose
to save her finger, his hacksaw kissing
the white gold band just below where
the bee had perched, confused, my father
said, by my mother's sweetness. The buzz
of the bee, the rasp of the saw raised
a horrible racket in my mother's ears,
but she couldn't lift her hands to cover them,
"hold your hand still, Bertie," my father said,
intent over the rise and fall of the blade,
the flesh on either side of the constricting band
white as a boil, the rest of the finger red
as a sausage. Afterwards, one half of the ring
was kept in my mother's jewelry box, its story
taking the place of the other half. There was
no explanation for what had become of it or how
my father was able to cut the ring without injuring
my mother's finger, or how either of them
had felt, my father on his knees in a caricature
of proposal as he ravaged the ring he had worked
so hard to get her, my mother frantic with pain
and fright, or so I imagine. Sometimes she
would take that broken arc of gold from its box
and hold it in her warm hand and we children
would beg for the story. If my father was
around, he would make a joke: *it was either
the ring or the finger, the ring or the wife,
and we could always get another ring,*
but for the rest of her life my mother wore
no ring and she never would say if
they'd made the right choice.

Something Lost

I am translating a poem by Margoshes.
He is a Cancer, and when the moon
is in the third quadrant of Jupiter he dreams
in Latin, a language he flunked in high school.
His teacher, a sadist named Wedick,
once humiliated him in front of the class,
remarking: "Latin's already a dead language,
there's no need for you to drive nails in its coffin."
Still, he dreams in Latin when there is fever
in the stars. Waking, the dream already a blur,
Margoshes rushes to the computer, which
has slumbered through the night dreaming
in machine language. He coaxes the dream out,
translating it into a poem in French, a language
he flunked in college, though Madame Chinard
was no Wedick, her humiliations more nuanced.
It falls to me, finally, to translate them into English.
From language to language, the images tumble,
resisting interpretation, giving up their meaning
with reluctance. My art is to tease these meanings
from their tangle, breathe life into them, make them
shine. What is it Margoshes means, what exactly?
It is to me the burden falls, translating opaque
into transparent. Still, something's always lost
in translation, some thing found only in dream.

The Clearing

I was writing a novel. I'd lost my job, stayed home.
We lived in a clearing carved out of wood, first by a river,
then by stubbornness. The fortunes of oil went up and down,
and now our neighbours' houses had gone empty, populated
only by the interest of bankers. I sat by a green window
in peace, and wrote, the dog asleep at my feet, while outside
our road vibrated like a violin string. The moose came out
of the trees, a yearling heifer, innocent of the steel ways
of the world. She came to the window and looked in as I
looked up, and only I was startled. She gazed at me as if I were
a Christmas display. I sat very still listening to the pulse
in my temple, felt the rotations of the planet around the sun,
the thrum of air against itself in the cycling wind, could hear
the sigh of time. I blinked many times and still she gazed at me,
devouring me with curiosity or near-sightedness, I couldn't say.
Eventually, she nodded in satisfaction, or so it seemed,
and lumbered off. Just then the dog woke, sniffed the air,
growled, barked. From a long way away came a reply.
Between where I sat and where my observer had stood
the thin membrane of glass blushed with the heat
of our encounter, the frothy air above me staggered
drunkenly. I bowed my head and wished her safe passage
in a world not made for innocence, curiosity, near-sightedness.

Passage

Driving up, I missed the turn, went right
through Watson without noticing the clamour
of signs, the traffic-cop hand of the elevator,
the gap-toothed grin of the Dairy Queen, found
myself in a new place, the landscape familiar
and foreign all at once. The time to be where
I was heading passed and still I drove, the road
a relentless passage into the unexpected,
unforgiving. I pulled over to consult the map,
turned around, the better part of an hour lost
in each direction but no real harm done.
Real time, the real place I was heading to
with all my vague intentions, a destination
now never quite to be achieved, some part of me
still hurtling north even as my body settled
into the expected routine of west.

Smiling faces crowd round as I slide out
from under the wheel, "So you got yourself
lost," my father says, a wink obscuring
his vision of me. In a year's time
he'll be dead. He takes my hand. "Well,
no harm done." Time lost but no harm.
Just another turn.

Athabasca Street

The retirement villa and the funeral home
sit tooth and jowl on a street called Athabasca,
a master stroke of urban planning. Someone
at the town hall has a grim sense of humour.
I stop in at the former to visit an aged uncle,
give the latter a wide berth, thinking
the *latterer* it be the better.

I find my uncle in a sunlit room, stirring
gnawed pits of cherries in a bowl, gazing
through a window at what I take to be
the middle distance. Given his age
and circumstances, he seems as well and fit
as can be. I ask him how he finds it here.
"Better'n next door," he tells me.

Railroad Flat

The Harlem Express shuddered by, indifferent
to the cinders it let fly into your eyes,
a thousand miles an hour, a thundering blur
of graffiti desire on the 3rd Avenue El,
a jumped-up elongated supernova
hissing its way across the sky, sunrise
to sunset and back again, dawn to dusk
to dawn a hundred times a day. The milk run local,
though, rattled to a stop right above my bed
all night long, a pulse in my temple. I heard
the pneumatic doors vacuum open and closed,
the erotic clamp of memory in my sleepless ear,
straining to catch a shout of laughter,
whispered gossip of morning. At some point,
death moved into the flat below, eternity
still skittering across the sky above, me pasted
breathless to the silent sheets.

Ashes

When the doctor told him they would kill him,
my father threw the open pack of Kools
from his pocket into the glove compartment
of his old Dodge Dart, where they stayed, temptation
and comfort. After his death, I empty the glove box,
shake one withered finger from that yellowed pack
and light it, though I gave up smoking myself
a few months ago. In the stale bitter smoke
that assaults my lungs, I taste my father's love
one last time. His death was a triple play: cold
to pneumonia to emphysema, out.

For years, taking the train to the city and back
every day, he had ridden in the smoking car,
breathing in its poison the way a man might inhale
a lover's perfume. Yet he'd remained faithful
to the pledge he took. In his hospital bed, he leaned
into my ear to whisper a plea, not for one last smoke,
as I expected, but to end his life, one wish
I could not grant.

Now I draw in the menthol smoke myself, as if I
were drawing life from his lungs, my own lungs
burning. Another puff or two, then I snuff out
the ember end with my fingers, welcoming
the small sting. I skin the last smoke, take its innards
in the palm of my hand, dry and granular
as broken ash. When I feel ready, I step out of the car,
walk into the copse of trees near the garage
and scatter my father's remains.

The Quilt

My grandmother plucks down from her geese
with fingers coarsened by kitchen, field and barn,
a snowstorm of feathers to be corseted
into thick ticking, sewed tight against
the long journey to come.

She has no time to teach her children,
that's dreamers' work for the beggars
at the door, former students of her husband,
fled to America. Bread and milk, eggs
and chicken, children cannot live on words,
it's fare for the passage that's needed.

A century later the quilt lies on my bed,
heavy as history.

At the National Yiddish Book Center

We go to Amherst to visit the Dickinson home
and find it closed, not yet 5 on a hot summer day
but already the small parking lot is deserted,
looking in its frilly maple coat more like something
from Frost than Emily. A page in our guidebook
mentions a Yiddish library at the nearby college,
and we drive over to take a look. The building hulks
against its landscape all shoulders and shrug
and splintery wood, designed, we read, to simulate
a *shtetl*, one of those Jewish villages wiped off
the map of Eastern Europe by war and design.
Inside, artful displays behind glass and a cavernous
sunken room filled with books. Finding they have
a copy of my grandfather's autobiography brings
the place into sharp focus. I have a copy myself,
on a high shelf at home, but I haven't held it
in years. It's in Yiddish, and I can't read it, his story
as opaque to me as the sheet of polished steel
behind a mirror's glass.

But here, inhaling the dust of the stacks,
I'm struck by how much the old man whose photo
fills the title page looks just like my father did
when he died, though my father is as long dead now
as *his* father was then, the ribbons tying us all
together, like the bookmark of frayed cloth sewn
into the binding, turning back on themselves,
unraveling. I am standing in a tunnel formed
by ceiling-high racks of books written in a language
almost as dead as my father, his father
and all their fathers and grandfathers before them,
nothing Emily Dickinson could have understood
though her hymns rang with the same cadences.
I hear them sounding a murmur in my ear,
a familiar whisper, a surging of blood.

Walking by Gibraltar Point Lighthouse in Moonlight

My first night on the island and I can't sleep. I creep from my room, from the darkened building, and follow the moonlight trail to the lighthouse, looming and sombre in its stone darkness, its light long ago extinguished. I've heard tales and I hope to meet a ghost, the spirit of Jimmy Rademuller, wayward keeper of the light, who disappeared one night in 1815, beaten to death by drunken soldiers, the story goes. He's said to walk here still, rattling the lock on the lighthouse door. If not Rademuller, than perhaps I'll come across the Bambino himself, Babe Ruth, who hit his first homer here, clear out of the stadium at Hanlan's Point and into the drink, over ninety years ago. He dreams of it even now, as we all dream of our first loves. Or Ned Hanlan, the great rower, whose statue greeted me when I stepped off the ferry, his restless eyes forever scanning his beloved bay. Any one of those ghosts would be welcome, so I am not afraid when I hear a step, a sigh, a great in-taking of breath, and feel a presence. I look up again at the implacable lighthouse wall no mortal man could climb, then turn easily, as if someone has called my name, although I know no mortal lips have formed it. I'm ready for the ghost, settled in my bones and skin for whatever may come.

But it's not Rademuller, not Ruth nor Hanlan, I see that in a flash. Rather a couple, strolling on the beach, hands clasped, she in long flowered skirt, he in his cap, bowlegged and shambling. I recognize them immediately, Gwendolyn MacEwen, who was librarian at the school here years ago, and Milton Acorn, who lived in a shack up the beach, even then a shipwreck of a man. Her eyes flicker to me and I think at first her glance is forlorn, but then see it as the hopeful resignation of exasperated love. Sunk in his own regard of himself, he seems unaware of my presence. I hear her placid "Milt," his high-pitched island "Gwen," and then they are gone and it's only the mumble of water against rocks I hear, only the signature of the moon I see across the lake's open face. From its great height, the lighthouse regards me with disinterest.

Poetry Lesson

Stone. Heart. Bones. Light. These are the words
we are told to avoid, our poems already filled
with them. The critics grow cranky. Better
to nurture our poems with science, politics,
DNA, sex, let them drown in their own sea
of language. But go ahead, open a vein, spill
your fecund blood on barren ground, let
a thousand flowers bloom, a thousand stars
implode, filling our worlds with crepe paper
darkness. Take dynamite to your poems, set them
ablaze. Let them rattle – oh, go ahead and say it –
in their bones. Take heart from this. Carve
your poems in stone, smooth stone, fill them up
with light, dazzling light.

Total Eclipse

It's easy to see how early man fell for the chicanery of religion.
Consider the eclipse of the moon, the rape of one celestial body
by another, the sun giving in to its most basic instincts
and devouring the object of its desire whole. Now think
of some poor besotted caveman, some half-breed Egyptian
or Assyrian or rune-addled Celt, with nowhere to turn but
up, nothing to believe in but the unthinkable. Every day more
or less the same, the seasons with their comforting rhythm
regular as breath, the cycle of day and night so dependable.
Then this unexpected carnage in the heavens, even stars
shocked into silence, seeming to confirm all those rumours
of Zeus and the mysterious others high in the mountains,
distant, unreachable. What else could it be? Even now,
with science behind us, the eclipse last night sent shivers
along our spines, reminding us there's more than one reason
to bend one's knee, to whisper prayers.

A Feeling

A feeling of hollowness comes over evening
after aluminum afternoons, as if we have become
the bones of birds. A feeling of electricity
when skin abrades skin, that nylon stocking
feeling, the snap of elastic garter. The copper
morning feeling, the cold cast iron of night, all
the metallurgy of the live-long day, that inside-
out feeling of never letting go. A feeling I get
standing next to you, your radiating heat, your
eyes seeing right through me. You know the feeling
I mean – that you could live forever, stay awake
forever, drive through the night on fries and shakes
and the scent of lilac. A feeling just before first light
of morning when you are too tired to think, too tired
to sleep. You stand by the window and watch the day
begin to settle into itself, assume the shape of desire.
A feeling to that shape, one you know so well.
You turn away from the window, then back to it.

Cancer

I'm a cancer, born in July,
never gave it a thought. Having
cancer, something else entirely.
I imagine this crab, all claws
and sly eyes, crawling inside
me, grinning mercilessly, making
her nest of bone and bits
of undigested flesh, dreaming
her own parasitic dreams.
Should I name her, this new pet
of mine, set out bowls of warm milk,
nurture a relationship? Do crabs
like to be petted? What *do* they like?

I think of the crabs I've eaten,
soft shell, cold legs in salad,
whole Chesapeake Bay crabs,
all you can eat, served dockside
in Maryland with nutcrackers,
mallets and paper bibs, coleslaw
and fries, plenty of cold beer.
How could a pleasure so pure
come back to haunt me except
as indigestion? Surely the crabs
I've eaten have shared my joy, given
themselves up gladly. I do not,
will not. This crab must dine alone,
shuttered in darkness, far from
the sea and company of its kind.
I shed no tears for its plight,
no more than it does for mine.

Suddenly Old

Tuesday, and I am suddenly old. I think
of phone calls unanswered over the years,
discontinued conversations, letters bravely begun
then abandoned. What to do with the broken-hearted,
torn leaves carpeting the ground after the storm?
Some songs refuse to be forgotten, stubborn
as chewing gum, as laughter. What was so
goddamned funny after all? Tuesday, Wednesday,
old. The face of a lover indelible as rain, her name
gone to sand. Mother's song, father's anger.
Putting down the dog you loved the most.
The kindest goodbye, the vet said. Yes, kindest.
But goodbye. Wednesday, Thursday, suddenly old.

The Body Politic

The body in rebellion against itself,
in argument, bloated with gas and anxiety,
valves rasping and leaking, corner joints
stiff with rust, full of protestation,
indignation, indigestion. On the outside,
shimmering skin, the curve and petulance
of sex, the surprising Herculean green
of an opened eye. Hair abundant, rich
as olive oil. Inside, unimaginable
darkness, humidity, fervour, rancour.
The body in revolt against its own edicts,
its own imprecations against imperfection,
intimations of mortality. At the centre,
the certain knowledge the centre cannot hold.

The Terrible Hour

Opening the door, you catch a glimpse
of endless waiting, a dark corridor of blood,
hear the faint echo of a howl. The moon
so bright you see the bones under your skin,
the face of the man in the moon
your own face, contorted with laughter.
This is the hour of the uncertainties,
the vague distance. You are standing
on a corner in cold rain waiting for a streetcar,
a cigarette in your lips, the match too wet
to strike. The iron taste of rain, blood again.
You strike the match over and over, until
it becomes memory. There's satisfaction
in knowing what happens next.

In Hospital

A hospital bed is the cruelest venue.
You lie there unable to sing or dance,
your thinking cloudy. All night long,
lights never really off, you flicker through
sleep like the phantom you might well
have become, one slip of the surgeon's knife,
while a chorus line pantomimes its way
through morphine dreams. Mornings,
daylight lays a fresh coat of grey paint
across ceiling and walls as the incessant hum
rises, the poke in the arm and the catheter's
relentless tugs the only reminders you're still alive
until the breakfast wagon rolls in. Another day
to contemplate mortality or the eternity
of whatever subject comes to mind. Then,
just like Jones, along come the surgeons, a trail
of them behind one shining star, nodding his head
like the Pope, inspecting his handiwork, the postulants
nodding their heads in agreement. This is the moment
around which the day revolves, freedom or another day
pinned to the bed hang in the balance, the jangle
of the IV machine just background music.
This moment, into which the leading man steps,
your life completely in his hands, next to the scalpel.

The Scar

My scar speaks to me in the night
in the language of torn muscle and gut.
It complains of fractures and fissures,
loss of modesty, holds me responsible.
It tells me, bitterly, how lucky I am
to have it and nothing worse. It's right,
of course, but...forever? The scar, reading
my thoughts, replies yes, till death do us part,
in a tone of malevolent humour. I'm woken
repeatedly by its singing a tuneless dirge,
as if to lull its own wounded self into numbness.
I hear it muttering under its breath, a faint whisper
droning on. Unable to sleep, I think
of the scar's accusation: that I am as much
a blemish on it as it is on me. I finger the raised
angry flesh, and my touch seems to calm
it. Soon it is silent, while I lie awake considering
the implications, for better or worse.

Still Life

Thursdays I do laundry.
Every day, walk the dog,
sing to the vines
on the upstairs landing.
Summers, tend the lawn
and garden, visit the graves.
Winter's another story,
a hard fable with the fire
to stoke, pictures to dust.
The dog settles, the teapot
steams its love song
to the passing train,
I close my eyes, listen
to legends told
by falling snow.
Nights go on forever.
Mornings, I rise
to the blessing of coffee,
of plums.

On Reading "Old Men, Smoking" by Sandra Kasturi*

He remembers the shape the smoke formed within
him, a cat stretching. He remembers his own shape
too was shifted, that people turned away as if they
heard something in the middle distance or remembered
something other than the person hoving into view,
wraithed in smoke, stinking of its wry perfume. He
remembers how the smoke had its way with him, cat
on a bird, how the taste turned to funeral ash on his tongue,
how the bitter cough became the better part of whatever
valour he may once have had, snubbed out. So many years
later – almost 30 is it? – he can still feel the firm roll
between his fingers, smell the burst of sulfur, feel
the heat, the fullness in his ancient blood. A fullness
shrunk to nothing, hollowness moving within him,
sideways, like a cat.

*as published in *Arc*

My Father's Ghost

More than thirty years dead, my father visits me
still in dreams. The other morning, his voice
was in my ear when I woke, the words fading
too quickly to catch his meaning. All day
I struggled to bring them back, but I might as well
have been netting gossamer. Another night, I
was startled awake by a presence in the room,
and thought I glimpsed him standing at the foot
of the bed, but looking away. I remembered
that deep night in the hospital, the life being choked
out of him, when he begged me to kill him and I
looked away – a lifetime as a son distilled
to that one terrible moment of failure. What did he
think of me then, that *I* wasn't worthy of his love?
Or did he feel a grudging respect? Unlike my father,
I have no son, no one to visit my final days,
for me to put in that awful spot. And like him,
when the time comes, I'll be alone.

Always Darkness

I sit on a park bench in the weak sun that follows
rain. Cooing pigeons resting in the cracks
of an old stone building behind me blur
into murmured prayer, in which I hear
the voice of my mother, her long-ago death
so recently observed. She is telling me,
through the obliging voice of a pigeon,
to be wary, that my own death is not far behind
the recollection of hers, though she
cannot foretell the time or circumstances.
Don't be afraid, she says. When I regain
my composure, I ask her, or I think I do,
*is there always light, as I've heard some people
say? No*, she answers, *darkness, always darkness.*
With pigeons shouting hosannas behind me
I see darkness too is a form of light.

Bird in the Hand

A small dark speck of cloud
detaches itself from the sky
like a disembodied leaf
taking leave of its tree
and presents itself, a gift,
to my open hand.
To my surprise, the bird
doesn't melt into air
but holds its ground, I feel
the grip of its feet, see
the diamond of its eye as it
cocks its head, taking me in.
I feel the pinprick of its beak
as it darts its head down
to seize the dried fruit I've
offered, feel its beating heart
against my skin radiating
through nerve and vein
to my own heart, hear the rustle
of feather and hollow bone.
For one long sweet moment
I'm as held by the bird
as it is by me.

The Heart in its Dotage

The heart in its dotage has eccentricities. It's partial
to blindfolded crosswords, walnuts in bed,
the jangled memory of crows at the darkest hour.
At this stage of its life, the heart sings out of tune,
dances a lame-footed jig, refusing to look back.
A hard-driver, a ripsnorter, a bellweather,
a dump-truck gigolo, a motherfucker, the heart is
the flickering light at the head of the stairs.

The heart, *this* heart, is the sum of all its varied parts,
the distance between zero and minus 60, the speed
of light slick on a polished floor. The *abiding* heart
takes a deep, stuttering breath, a long last glance,
calculates the odds on its fingers. The ripened heart's
hearing is going, it has to stop, ask directions. The heart
is failing in its dotage, yes, but it remembers everything.

Focus

There comes a time, finally,
when you see the world
for what it is: a memory.
The air in its shimmering skin,
sunlight diaphanous in its,
and you in your own, all
rutted and plain, but comfortable
enough, at peace with the resolution.
You note the lens through which you
see all this requires one more twist
of the knob, just the slightest
of adjustments.

2

Topsy-Turvy

I'm as full of shit as the next guy.
— painter Michael Goldberg

The Poem Seduces the Poet

This poem says no. It bucks and mewls
like a mustang, digs in its heels, refuses
to play along. Brooding. it muses
and fusses, shoots me glances dark enough
to curdle my blood. The poem mutters
under its breath, whines, sits on its haunches
and howls to the moon.

But later, the poem takes a deep breath
and makes a new commitment, vowing
to behave, to live up to expectations.
It smiles, slips into something comfortable,
dabs perfume behind its ear. It's preparing
a nice dinner, putting a good white wine
on ice. It has plans for me.

Cool

Two dead guys walk into a bar.
They get their drinks fast* but
don't take the hint, stay all night,
eating peanuts, joking with the barmaid.
They stay forever, give the place a bad name.
The neighbourhood changes, business
goes in the toilet. Eventually there's
a new owner, redecoration, a theme. They
pull down the old sign, haul up the new,
"Two Dead Guys Holding Court."
They're the silent partners, the big draw,
give the place a certain, oh,
Je ne sais quoi. There are write-ups
in the papers and a better class
of clientele starts slipping back, word
gets around, those dead guys are OK,
they're cool.

* from a poem by Susan Stenson

This Train Don't Carry No Gamblers

It takes a lot to laugh,
It takes a train to cry – Bob Dylan

The train in the night is a woman, her stunted heart bent...no, start again. The train in the night is an abandoned child, hungry in its crib...no, no, too obvious. Again. The train in the night is an animal, twisting in its furrow....no, no, for God's sake, no. Tormented souls of the departed, no, definitely not. The memory of factories, no, the loneliness of cities, no. No, no. The train in the night is...a train... in...the night! Isn't that enough?

        Darkness falls, over a far land, empty and treeless, lit only by impossibly distant stars and the underbellies of clouds, still cold from winter. Through all this huffs the train, sleek and lethal, filled with its own form of emptiness. It has traveled for a long time, its passengers weighed down with their own sad stories, their own reasons. When it opens its mouth and screams, it is only itself, unadorned.

Scare Crow

Straw man at my door this morning.
His tattered suit one I gave away years
ago. I catch a reflection of myself
in the elbow's shine, so much pain
in my eyes. His grotesque head
an old sock stuffed with other old socks,
festooned with button eyes, button nose
and ears, zipper mouth, an open mouth
filled with straw and invective. A broken
broomstick holds this contraption together,
broomstick up an ass of straw. He begins
to berate me, pointing the flaccid finger
of an empty old glove at the hollow
of my chest. Curses fill his mouth
but straw can only convey so much.
Scares the crow right out of me
just the same, the crow, the raven,
the raucous magpie, a flock of waxwings
springing from my startled mouth,
bohemians and hosannas.

At the Debutantes' Ball

The trees wear their hearts on their sleeves
tonight, and babble about lost loves, heartbreak,
stunted youth. They deck themselves out
as debutantes always have, a bit too revealing
for the older generation's approval, gaudy enough
to satisfy each other's envy. Their own exhalations
have clouded the sky, pulling a veil over stars
and the *tut-tutting* moon. These debs really couldn't
care less. Days of reckoning lie ahead, they
know, but these are salad days, a whole rich copse
of pleasure opening before them, a verdant clearing
in which they will always be young.

Armstrong's Foot

Blake's fearsome tyger
stuffed and raffled off
on the midway, Johah's whale
a cartoon pitch
for tuna. The snake
in the garden just a torn strip
of inner tube after all, the moon
when Armstrong's foot left
its mark nothing more
than the green cheese
my grannie always said
it would be, cheese
filled with holes.

Topsy-Turvy

Tomato basil soup for lunch, made
by Rosemary. Or is it tomato rosemary
soup, made by Basil? Everything
is topsy-turvy here, trees talk
to each other, blossoms on the vine
quiver, listening. The sky turns
itself inside out, showing us its fleece,
begging for mercy. Painters here
are colour blind, singers deaf. Dancers
are everywhere, their feet made of lead,
yet still they fly. Priests are sinners here,
lawyers criminals. Birds strut on surprising
stilts and men slither on their bellies, seeking
redemption. Yes, that much is the same.
But there is no redemption. Gods
worship men here, and soon lose
their religion.

A Prayer at Sunset

This is a prayer made of dry leaves,
a prayer of rotted blossoms,
sour cut grass. This is a prayer
of stagnant water where mosquitoes
breed, prosper and die
in a recurrent buzz
that ends only with a slap.
You are on your knees, your head
bowed, considering mortification
of flesh, transmogrification
of souls. This is a prayer *of* the flesh,
of spirit extinguished,
of the connection between
the palm of your right hand
and your naked upper left arm,
the only thing between them
that aggravating rasp.
This is a prayer
of the last gasp,
religion laid bare.

The Fortune Cookie

The fortune cookie is an oyster protecting
its pearl, the pearl a secret dying to be told.
For something so innocuous, the shape
of the cookie is sumptuous, all curve
and lip in its crinkly cellophane. You hold it
to your ear and it whispers your name above
the growl of surf. You eat the cookie only
as an afterthought, its aftertaste sweet
or bitter, depending on the message.
And that's what it comes down to, isn't it?
On one side, the cryptic message – surely
what it says can't be what it means – or
can it? On the other, a series of numbers,
faint as an ancient tattoo, that never add up.
Still, the balance of words on one side
and numbers on the other, neither conveying
any truth, yields a certain trivial pleasure. Slick
now with soy sauce from your fingers, the strip
of paper is light as a feather in your hand.
You read the message again, count the numbers,
place a morsel of cookie on your tongue. Again,
it whispers your name, and something else.

Poet, Seeking an Audience

The wind sloughing through the firs speaks
in tongues, boasting of its pregnant coat
of snow, of the burdens it carries, the honey
in its puckered cheeks. The rhymes it makes
are too complicated for the normal ear,
the prosody of its song too subtle. Dogs
pick up their heads and follow along,
entranced by a rhythm only they can hear.
The wind is a braggart, a – well – a blowhard,
full of itself, so sure, so intemperate.

Thirteen New Ways, with One More for Luck

From the Coke machine, a blackbird, rattling
its beak like a hammer. Darkening the moon,
a pair of blackbirds, so smug. In a phone booth,
a trio of blackbirds, eavesdropping party lines,
killing themselves with laughter. They are
everywhere, these silhouettes, inflections
and innuendoes, a quartet of black velvet cutouts
on the refrigerator door, inkspots on a blotter,
five of them lurking in the mouth of an alley,
weighed down by gold chains and knuckle dusters,
a sestet of them in the one place you might
actually think to look, power lines, holding on
for dear life in a cuckold wind. Seven of them,
larger than life, indecipherable, on stamps,
collectors' issue, ringed in gold, eight on the labels
of *shmatas* from Hong Kong. Nine blackbirds
all in a row, one of them slightly plumper
than his fellows, boisterous at a wedding table,
licking their chops. Ten of the bloody blighters
at sea in a leaky rowboat, with a cow, a spoon,
a tarnished teakettle. One less a dozen washing
their faces in muddy puddles drunk as lords,
writing poems, baying at the moon. A full dozen
on the back of the new ten-dollar bill, oily blots
on a napkin. Everywhere, these birds, a baker's
dozen, yes, thirteen, so unlucky, circling
the graveyard, their shadows forming templates
for deaths yet to come, fourteen in a hayloft,
just one with a needle hidden in its feathers. It's
the one you need to watch out for.

> – After "Thirteen Ways of Looking at a Blackbird"
> by Wallace Stevens

An Aviary of Song

The song of the disparaging sparrow is a monotonous one,
its fault-finding relentless. The gull's song is religious:
give me fish, he cries, *and I will feed multitudes.*
The robin's song is a menu: feed *me*, it commands.
Practical bird, with a family to consider, it has
little interest in music, only stuffing its flamboyant shirt.
The meadowlark's song is another matter. In the meadow,
it improvises; by the slough, it falls back on what it knows:
rhythm, rhyme, syncopation. Slowly, the concept
of melody evolves, thought percolating through mud.
A solitary meadowlark is a clarinet on a deserted street.
Two meadowlarks a bebop reunion. More than three,
Pachelbel's Canon, complete with choir. From its perch
high above, the envious magpie looks on, contemplating
the absence of song, lighting the fuse with its glowing cigar.

Salvation

Like an image on paper in a chemical bath
my life snaps into focus as I roll home
on clouds, their silver linings held close
to God's chest. Frugal with His blessings
and revelations, He loves to tantalize, keep
us in suspense: heaven or hell, redemption
or damnation dealt out with the cool
indifference of a card shark.

I live a good life, I do good, but I have
my own secrets. I was mean
more than once. Will that be enough
to keep me outside? Some would wish me
there forever, hating me for the predictable
reasons. It's their certainty that *I* hate.

But stars are out tonight and it's possible
to imagine they are gold fillings
in God's mouth. Is he smiling or yawning?
Smiling, I think. Yes, smiling.

Modern Life

The egg is a lonely traveller.
Will she be a chicken? No thank you,
she says. Ah, a meal then! Scrambled, fried,
poached....? No thank you again, if it's all
the same to you. The egg is very polite. She
also declines omelet, soufflé, quiche,
more elegant but just as fatal. An egg
can't be too careful. An egg must think
of all possibilities, examine her options,
take no sides. The past faces her from
all directions, likewise her future. Yet
she must consider her future: go
with the flow, roll with the punches, avoid
the bumps. The one thing she need not do is
watch her diet: her shape is one thing she has
little care for. She is too self-possessed
for that, too self-contained. She appreciates
the admiring glances she gets, dismisses those
who are disrespectful. She refrains from making
obvious puns. An egg longs to be held, cool
and grave, in the palm of her lover's hand,
to be rolled along the soft skin of his cheek.
She has hardened her own skin but her heart
can be broken.

New York City Summer

Bottles rattle their bones in the alley,
a tomcat syncopation as pleasing to the ear
as a Brubeck break into five/four time,
that dazzling left hand. Garbage trucks
hum their own tune, an off-key melody
patched together from scraps. The song
of the city rises with the tincan perfume,
the heat of the day before still holding us
like a child with an injured bird cupped
in her hand. Soon enough that hand will close,
choking us, sending us out onto the fire escape,
the roof, the sizzling street, seeking solace,
the cool glance of the passer-by. All day long,
sun's white-hot poker, all night long,
the long slow hiss.

Square Dance of the Trees

Hot summer nights, in the neon moonlight,
the trees in my backyard get up to dance.
They shake the lethargy from their limbs,
stretch their branches, arc their trunks, let
their backbones slide. Great roots of feet
glide across the moss as if they were
cushioned on air and the earth trembles,
just for a moment, then settles itself
to a steady thrum. The elm, the hawthorn,
the crabapple, the plum, move around
the garden with stately grace as I sleep,
bowing to each other, *do-si-do and around
you go*, light as wisteria, delicately breathing
in each other's blossoms. There is romance
under the moonlight, as might be expected,
and the occasional flash of jealousy. As the moon
swings low in the sky and the stars pale, the dancers
shamble to the fence lines and become wallflowers
surprised by their boldness. Dawn creeps
in, flooding the yard with light and sun
and soon I appear, with coffee cup
and paper, stepping out onto grass still fresh
with dew. I stand motionless, eyes patrolling
fence, trees and shrubbery, the innocent flowers
in their borders. Something seems amiss,
something, perhaps, out of place, and I catch
a flurry of motion, just a suggestion,
in the corner of my eye.

Dreams of a Snowy Evening

The flea dreams of the dog, the dog
of hearth and fire. Fire dreams
of winds rushing down a chimney, seducing
it into something greater than itself.
Its nightmare is rain. The chimney dreams
of both the firm hand of the mason
and the sweep, the two great loves
of her blackened life. The sweep dreams
of his broom, the mason, fitfully, of the stone
he could not lift. The sculptor too dreams
of that stone, of the shape he would make
of it if only he could. The stone dreams
of rain, the rain of moss, the moss of fire,
and round we go again, fire, hearth, dog,
flea. All the while, wide awake, snow falls.

Thirty-Nine Kinds of Light*

Skittering across snow.
Filtered through trees, apple in full leaf.
Dappled on moving water, amidst the singing.
Buttery on a field of wildflowers.
Shining on butterfly wings.

Piercing the otherwise impenetrable night,
    the sky showing its teeth.
A saint's hand, offered through cloud.
Waxing.
Waning.
Undecided in its sly grin and in its full promise.

Black glow of eclipse after furious rain.
Slicing through sea's green flash of phosphorescence.
Aurora borealis, the sky showing off.
A fire in the distance.

A volcano's throbbing ash, mountain with a toothache.

Dawn's gleaming.
Morning's sullen grey, brightening.
High noon's lustrous pearl.
Sunset red, the ache that follows.
Evening's last lingering pulse, the sigh.
Cigarette glowing in an empty room.

In the hair of a newborn child.
In your eyes, looking at me now.

The radiance of a new mother.

A solitary stroke of lightning.

Current sizzling the heavens.
Lightning bugs in dance.
Electric eels in love.

Muted, in a steam bath.
Naked, above the operating table.
Glinting on the edge of a knife.
Freight train on a trembling trestle.
Relentless elucidation.

Through a newly washed window,
through smoke, slowly,
through fog, tiptoeing,
through lightly falling rain.

In good Scotch whisky.
In a painting by Monet.

*"One of the most obvious examples is [Crozier's] use of 'light,' which
by my count makes 39 appearances in only 61 poems. And this is only
considering instances of the word itself, not taking into account
dozens of other manifestations in the form of sun, stars, moon, and
various other gleamings, glintings, shinings, and glimmerings."

– Zach Wells, *Quill & Quire*

Dictionary of Small

There is a dictionary of small things.
It contains hummingbirds and rubies,
pituitary glands and walnuts, avocados,
amethysts, azaleas. There are
wedding bands, smooth pebbles
from a creek, invitations in their creamy
envelopes, a leftover rose. No corsages,
though – too big. The editor is strict
about this, nor will he accept things
that are too small to see, microbes, genes,
germs and the like. *Small* is what he has
in mind, small enough to fit comfortably
in the palm of one's hand. Paper clips,
but no tacks, peanuts, in the shell, chocolates,
glass eyes, spent or full cartridges, a gold coin
yes, a stuffed wallet no. He is considering
candidates now for the new edition, things
that change their shape: snowball,
candy apple, lumps on a breast, mercy.

3

The Ripening

Quinzee

(for Dave Carpenter)

Start with a snowball in your hand, an idea.
Shovel after shovel, the idea snowballs
into a parody of itself. This takes a day or two,
then stand back and inspect your handiwork,
a big Jesus pile of snow, rounded. Then get on
your knees and begin to dig. Think Holland Tunnel,
straight in, till you're absorbed. Snow muffles
sound and those outside think you've packed it in.
You have, but you haven't left and the scat of snow
you leave behind is your mark for those who can read
it. The cave grows larger in proportion to the thinning
of the walls, this much is physics. What goes beyond
science into art and religion is the light, light so delicate
you hate to cut into it, afraid it will shatter. Outside,
there is panic, you've been gone so long, days
without word except for the endless stream of snow
the tunnel disgorges. The warmth of the snow leaches
into the close air around you, suffocating. You eat
snow, drink your own sweat. You know that all
the bad jokes are starting to come true, you're
growing younger, sliding backwards into the womb,
with that final shovelful you'll be reborn.

Creation Theory

(for Lorri Neilsen)

Break open a stone, water.
Tie water in a knot, stone.
Tie snakes in a knot, woman.
Break a woman's heart, man.

So the seasons cycle into one
another, causes abundant.
Break. Tie. Tie. Break. Down
through generations, smoke
clearing at last upon an Eden.

Atonement

We think of the apple,
but Eden was lined
with cinnamon trees,
an orchard of cinnamon
arranged in the shape
of a commandment.
In the garden's centre
grew nutmeg, vanilla,
cashew and quince.
After the fall, Eve
gathered up bushels
of the once-forbidden,
picked handfuls of flavours,
bound them in pastry,
seeking atonement.
She created an aroma
that lifted to heaven
in the form of a prayer.

Adam

There is an ache in my side
where the wife clawed her way
out, leaving her shadow
on my bones. There is an ache
in my chest over the anger
of my sons, an ache in my loins
for the implied daughters,
their grievances. There is an ache
behind my eyes left by what
I've seen and what remains
unseen, an ache in the palms
of my empty hands, tips
of my fingertips, so much left
to grasp. God made me a promise.
Yes, there is an ache there too.

Comfort

He woke to the sound of a woman crying
in the next room. No, it was further away, down
the hall, perhaps even on another floor. He was
certain he knew who it was, the attractive blonde
woman with blue nails he'd seen in the lobby
as he waited for the elevator. When the doors opened,
she hesitated and didn't get in. He remembered
thinking she was a woman who would soon be crying,
though he didn't know her, certainly knew nothing
of the sorrow living within her like a small animal
in the forest. Now she was crying – *someone* was,
some woman was crying – though as he listened harder
he realized he did not actually hear the crying, just
felt the sense of it. Yes, it was the blonde woman,
come to the end of something, alone in a hotel room
in a strange city, fearful even of the company
of an unexpected man on an elevator. He threw aside
the covers, rose from the warm bed and went
to the window, separating the heavy drapes. Far below,
the street, earlier filled with taxis, was empty,
glistening, as if rain had fallen or snow melted. He stood
framed in the window, naked for anyone who
might be watching to see, hoping that somehow
he was bringing her comfort.

Before Summer's Arrival

Early June I wake to the song of nightingales flooding
the neighbourhood, sweeten my coffee with decaying lilac,
sleepwalk through a somnolent day heavy with the dregs
of obligation and regret, a joyless but serene day
like the ones we endured at school. As the month deepens,
days become clues in a crossword puzzle I'm unable
to finish, air thins to the snapping texture of cellophane
and I lie naked on my restless bed with the window open
and allow the night to devour me. This is how I greet
summer, who has whispered promises in my ear all winter,
made staticky phone calls through bitter spring. I turn
my head to the window at the buzzing, a mosquito smaller
than the chimes of netting, bringing me a virus kiss
as a baroque gift. In the fever's flannel embrace I find
that I can fly, stumble silently through walls, see forever,
there is nothing beyond my reach or grasp. Drained, I sleep
finally while the sultry night spins in its own fever, baying
at the operatic moon. In the days before summer's arrival
I open myself to its promised possibilities, close my ears
to its stuttering denials. When it does arrive,
I can honestly say there are no secrets between us.
We are like man and wife, grown old in each other's breath,
the tumult of stars in summer's pulse, just silence in mine,
just silence.

Writing My First Book

They retired me from the plant so I thought I'd write a book. The boys at work always said I should, no one could spin a yarn like me, like that time at the Christmas party with Wilma and Joe, all those hijinx during the big strike. I bought a pen, a pad, made a desk of an old door and a pair of horses, sat down, waited for the muse to holler in my good ear. Ain't that what they say, you need inspiration? I made a pot of coffee, strong, like I read they do in Paris at them cafes, and drank it slow till it was cool in my little cup. Watched the sunset. Waited. After a while, when I couldn't think of nothin' else, I began to write about myself – ain't that some more good advice? Write about what you know, the feller said. With me, it's the plant, all those years, good and bad, and Gladyce, my life with her, likewise good and bad, though now, with her gone, it's the good I dwell on, the bad just makes me sour. And there's the kids, all grow'd up now, kids of their own, and the place at the lake we had for a while, more shack than cabin, and those times I lapsed, not making excuses but there they were, there they are. Can't help comin' back to them. But that's not the kind of thing you want to write about, is it? Well, maybe some do, but not me, and the other stuff, maybe not as interesting as I thought.

I mentioned all this to one of the boys I ran into at the Legion. He sez *whatcha been up to, you writin' that book?* And I tell him about the pencil and pad, the door between the horses, the waitin'. *Just don't you write nothin' 'bout me,* he sez, *that time during the goddamn strike when we all got a little crazy, don't let me see my goddamn name in any book you write.* Well, calm down, Harry, you won't.

No, I been sittin' here, watchin' sunsets and sunrises too, lettin' the coffee in my little cup cool, thinkin' about what I'd *really* like to write and it don't have nothin' to do with the plant, the boys and their hijinx, nothin' about the tools in the garage or that stamp collection I had when I was a boy. Don't worry, Harry, it's the lapses I keep comin' back to, like I said, but not yours. The fixes you got yourself into are your own affair, write your own damn book, man. With me, it's what I done, what I didn't do, that seems to matter after all. All the things I didn't do. And the ones I wisht I hadn't.

All Happy Families Are the Same

My father went to work in a suit, tie and hat,
yours in coveralls, but they played
poker together Saturday night, drank the same
beer. Both our mothers painted their nails
bright red, sipped sherry at parties, sang
off key. Our sisters were inseparable. But
your people were Republican, Catholic,
Knights of Columbus, mine Democrat,
Jew, Kiwanis. My father read Freud
in the bathroom, yours played baseball
with his sons until after dark and your mother
called them in. Our sisters had a falling out,
something about a boy. My sister's abortion,
your brother Tony's suicide, these things
we didn't talk about. This was years ago.
Both our mothers grew old before their time
and died, our fathers soon after. In the end,
they couldn't remember if they'd been happy.

A New Boyfriend

Shelley's new boyfriend stands
a little awkwardly as we size
him up, we will not let her go
lightly. Her house already up
for sale, everyone but the boss
knows she's leaving, we
already gave her the going-away.
It's hard to imagine this place
without her, the shape of absence
she'll make when she steps
out of her shoes, the ones
someone else will have the devil
of a time to fill. No one like her,
that girl, her smile, that flip
of her hair, the quick movement
of her hand, everybody says so.
She steps away and the space
she leaves begins to fill in,
the impression her presence left
swimming into focus like the image
on the Polaroid someone snapped,
the boyfriend to the side rather
than centred in the frame with her,
a bit awkward, as if he understood
the transience of his position. There is
a quickness to her step we haven't seen
before, then quickly the impression fades.

Advertisements for Ourselves.

"Her breasts no larger than mine..."
The first line from a poem called "Marilyn"
by dee Hobsbawn-Smith

We go out into the world in the bodies we inhabit,
advertisements for ourselves. Passing a mirror, you
might pause, startled by the unexpected stare back
of a stranger, the person you once were, the person
you might have become, even the person you might
already be, still growing into yourself, your future
undetermined. You might be a woman with breasts
smaller than you'd like or larger than you think
they should be. You see the eyes of men on you
and even those of other women, judging, comparing,
finding fault. Flipping through a magazine, you find
photos of a great beauty long dead and are surprised
to see her breasts little different than yours. When
you mention this to your friends, there is laughter,
whether at the brazenness of your boast or in the shock
of recognition, you cannot say. Is it the costumes
she wore, the photographer's art or the movies' sleight
of hand that makes her appear so much more
than she was, while you, in the naked light of day,
seem so much less? *Live fast, leave a beautiful corpse*,
she did that. You walk out into the world, shoulders back,
feeling the daily decay, the bewildering passage of time,
the ripening. Shoulders back, best foot forward.

Woman of the House

A woman kept in a house is like a cuckoo kept
in a clock.* Milk runs in her breasts like electricity,
the ringing of a phone. She hears a knock at the door,
the step of the postman, the refrigerator's harmony
with the moon. In the early hours, while the house
and children sleep, she rereads letters
from the latticed box on the closet shelf
by the blue television light. Did he really say
those things, ever mean them? All so long ago.
A woman kept in a house is like the kiss of a vacuum
on a pane of glass, the slow passage of time. All night
the house blows in the wind, a cradle.* The house reads
her like a pane of glass, the roughened braille fingers
of electricity, the urgency of milk. The phone
unanswered, the letters tucked away again.
So long ago.

* lines from a poem, "Purdah," by Jennifer Boire

Slipped Away

What she remembered about that night,
she told her children, was not the moon
agape in amazement or the brazen stars
or the drunken scent of lavender
in the June air, comforting as her own breath,
not the certain knowledge that someday
she would be telling them this, not the way
he spoke to her, though his manners were
courtly, nor the slightly askance look in his eye,
not the guitars tuning in their muffled cloister
or the brave hiccup of drums, the heart divided
against itself, the downcast eye, the mirage,
not the dream or the waking, or even
the delirious moment before sleep when all things
are said to be possible, no, what she remembered
was the pause, the slipping away into herself.

– after Neil Young's "Slip Away"

Rice

A wise man comes to the green river
and pauses to rest. Wise enough to go
no further, he bends his knee and gathers
water in his cupped hands, sits in the sun
until the water reaches its anticipated boil.
One grain of rice resides in his emaciated bag.
It is enough. Into the bubbling water
it happily goes, the purpose of its perfect life
almost achieved. Soon, stout with pride,
scented with humility, it is everything
it can or could be, and the wise man
falls to his feast, careful to leave a morsel
to appease both god and devil. Sated, he gazes
into the river until its flow ceases, for the river
too is wise, and he's allowed to cross. Then he
carries on until he reaches his destination.

Home

We built our homes on the barren plain
but dark winds, rain and fire drove us away.
We set up camp in woods, below trees and high
within their sheltering arms, but climbing snakes
and spiders and fierce-teethed cats attacked us.
We limped into caves, aware that our evolution
was against all sense of reason, but we were
caught up by forces stronger than expected, fissures
in the earth spitting like animals, belching heat,
floods that first saved us, then tumbled us
to within a breath of our lives. At dawn we woke
and the strong set out while the rest of us sank
into the crevices of earth's welcoming arms.

The sun beats down on us. Wind fans our fevered
skin, rain cools us and so, through the cycle
of the seasons we endure, waiting for some
fabled rescue. Slowly we realize we've found
what we sought. Looking around we take
comfort, shake our heads at our slowness.

Road to Janda's

Halfway up the railroad hill on the dust road to Janda's,
an abandoned farmhouse hangs loose as teeth
in a drunkard's mouth. Around back, a boarded-up well
rewarded the nets of queasy fishermen with the body
of a child years back, whether murder or accident
the story doesn't say. Afterwards, cattle took sick
and died, the tenants afflicted by madness, even
frogs in the pond grew silent, fish rolled their bellies
to the pallid sun and, strangest of all, there were no flies.

Even now, so many years later, no one recalls the names
of child or fishermen, kids on their skeletal bikes pause
in the dust to stare at the house's blind eyes, all glass
long gone, the shelterbelt withered from drought. There's
talk now of new housing up to Janda's, paving the road,
better times. Men in suits drive slowly by in slippery cars,
eying the dried-up pond, the crabgrass and purple thistle,
making calculations. They get out and walk about
like cautious tourists, brushing dust from their shirtfronts.
The sun is weak; no breeze, no shade, no flies.

Jesse James and His Men Settle Down

We entered Kansas as rapists and stayed as lovers.
Our intentions were the worst but our hands were
clean and we had open hearts. We fell in love
with Kansas, its wide-open horizontals, the secrets
of its verticals, its dark narrow places, so we stayed,
redeemed men with no memories to haunt us. Slowly,
the women returned, then the children from the places
they'd hidden, finally the livestock reappeared,
cattle, hogs, chickens. The rhythm of the place took on
a certain vigour. In the evenings, we stood by the window
watching, watching, until it was too dark to see.

The Day After

On September 12th, in Rayfield, Ohio, there were
flowers, hot coffee in the morning, cinnamon buns
and laughter as the cheerleaders collided with each
other exiting the yellow bus. Life went on in Rayfield
despite the terrible images everyone in town had seen
on television. People shook their heads, with disbelief,
with disgust. Not for a minute did any of them sit stunned
in silence in a school the way the President did in that film.
Across the street from the school an old man with a goiter
sat in a sway-back chair in front of the drugstore, smoking
a corncob pipe. He watched the cheerleaders and thought
about some things he'd seen in his long life: the mud
at Juno Beach clinging to his boots, the policeman
who came to his door late one night. He thought too about
the TV screen, the stories he'd read that morning in the paper,
and about his great-grandson, little Tommy, barely 5, what
he'd tell him that night when he held him in his arms, fresh
from his bath and ready for bed. All through the town
of Rayfield fathers were thinking about what they would tell
their daughters that evening, mothers their sons, husbands
their newlywed wives, all the same thing. Barbers were already saying
it with a shrug, whispering it into the chastened ears of the heads
their scissors moulded. Joan at the Payless checkout counter
spoke it to the woman in a flowered dress buying flour
and toothpaste. The woman nodded and repeated it. All across
Rayfield, Ohio, in the heart of the nation, people were saying it
or thinking of saying it. For this one moment, they spoke as one.

Last Days

in memory, Jay Scott

The prognosis was as bad as could be
and he walked home alone hearing
the bones of his legs rattle, drowning out
everything else. Flowers bloomed on his skin
and caves were discovered, waiting to be
explored. *It's the waiting*, he kept telling
people, *not what's at the end.* Within his knees
and wrists bones shouted at him, tendons holding
him together snapped, his lungs blackened
like a miner's. On Saturday, he and Robert
took the streetcar to the beach and walked
on the sand. *I'd swim out as far as I could
but I can't swim*, he said, and Robert wept.
Above them, seagulls wheeled and spun, calling
as if they'd seen something. One gull, emboldened,
swooped closer to whisper in his ear,
and he smiled knowingly. *Ah.*

Stars

There might have been music.
It may have been June, a warm night,
a verandah. The moon may have been
rising, not quite full of itself
in a cloudless navy sky made bright
by a cornucopia of stars.
There may have been dancing, I
may have taken you in my arms,
light as a down pillow, warm
as a comforter, the blonde hairs
on your arm electric, the scent
of you filling my breath. I may have
whispered something in your ear,
something that made you pull
back sharply, your eyes filled
with a reflection of yourself
in mine. There may have been
a small moment of regret.
All that is conjecture. What is
certain is the coldness of the stars.

Wisdom

A man walks to the edge of the pier and looks
into the bottomless sea; enamoured of the fishes
and their secrets, he knows not to jump in.
His brother opens the window on the 17th floor
the better to see butterflies and birds – *I could fly*,
he thinks, but he too resists the urge. All day long
we are tested by temptation and still we batter on
against the wind, glancing both left and right
yet aiming straight ahead. At day's end, we take off
our shoes, savour the anticipation of cool sheets,
steaming coffee in the morning, consolation enough.
There's wisdom in the stars if only we could see it.

Stephen Hawking in Saskatchewan

(for Gary Hyland)

Preposterous! Of course. But in a universe
of possibilities, a random universe
such as he himself has postulated,
no compelling reason why not. And here
he is in fact, striding across a swath
of native short grass prairie alive
with hoppers and bees, the heady scent
of pollen swirling around his shining head,
no wheelchair or other aid in sight.
A splendid figure of a man, square-jawed
and shouldered, golden-haired, his smile
a constellation of neon stars, a milky way
of attraction, unmovable, irresistible,
and, in a universe of possibilities, why not?

His gait, as he makes his way through sage
and wolf willow, tentative, yes, as if it has been
a long time since he stretched his limbs, but
his eye is practiced, his calf, when he pauses
to hike his pants' leg and scratch, muscular
as a sprinter's, stretched steely spring. But
what's this? Embedded in the hairy skin, a tick,
already swollen, a full moon of greed.
The tick's mouth is a valve, a nipple, burrowed
under the skin like a star consumed by its shadow,
swallowed by the black hole of its own need,
its body glossy with self-important possibility,
already predicting the final tenor of its arc,
desire, hunger, satiation, rest.

4

The Road Going On, or Feral Indirection

Another Road

The road going on – past the mailbox, past
the drive, the dip, the curve, the flaming stand
of lilac, all those familiar landmarks –
into unfamiliar territory. Why have we
never gone this way before? No map,
no clue, no desire. No presence of mind.
No one to ask. The road with its hum,
a hundred miles of whiskey timber road,
Marianne Faithful on the radio, that much
hurt. The night an envelope with no address,
splinters under your skin tattooing a heart
with a dagger on your bicep. All these marks,
these signs, all this feral indirection.

Two Months Adrift

I was asked to house-sit but arrived to find
the house had burned down, leaving ashes
and ghosts of the plants and cats I was to look
after. Still, I took my duties seriously and moved
through the detritus polishing furniture, tidying
up. Where the south window had been I opened
the curtains and let in the sun, admired
the bric-a-brac I imagined lining the sill:
glass elephants and a hula girl made
of toothpicks, her eyes bright as embers, a shell
from the Sargasso Sea. I held it to my ear
but heard only the raging flames. For weeks,
I waited for the letter, the phone call. When winter
came, I had no choice but to move on. I locked
the door, swept the stoop, left a forwarding address.

Silent Night

Even the stars have grown quiet tonight, quit
their constant gossip and prognostication,
their intergalactic screeching ebbed first
to throbbing chatter, then a hum, then just gone.
Silent. The moon and sun have shut their traps,
the seas murmuring only to themselves
in imagined tides. Trees have ceased
their anxious whispering and all the creatures
of this world, and the next, have fallen mute,
waiting for god to clear his throat
and begin the next chapter.

Darkness

"I have faith in nights," Rilke wrote, his eyes
on the great power he felt moving beside him.
He was a slender man alone on an endless horizon
where the chances of thicker men are better. Thick,
thin, the power he felt makes no distinction, leveling
all it comes across without bias or favour, pulling
everything into fire's bright circle of light, trumping
darkness. But Rilke's night, the darkness he came
from, endures, it gathers its own power, sees itself
through to dawn, when it's safe to shut its eyes.

> – After "You darkness," by Rainer Maria Rilke

Creation

God came back from a trip to the outer stars,
totally beat. For days, He loafed around Heaven
catching up on sleep, making jigsaws
of His design, restless in His own desire.
The angels kept out of His way. God thumbed
through The Book, nodding His head, shaking
His head, making notes. He had something
in the back of His mind.

Evolution

The amoeba curses its loneliness and splits, finds itself
at war with its other, in love. The worm defies the logic
of its head and allows its tail to wag itself into submission;
another split, another war, another torrid love affair.
The fish grows weary of water and sprouts wings, then,
disenchanted with air, learns to crawl on a belly full
of lesser species. Another bird seeks the peace
of rumination and becomes a cow, setting off
a trend, cow into horse, horse into dog, dog into cat, each
one seeking a more perfect self. Among the so-called higher
species there is debate that will later come to be known
as a roomful of Jews arguing theology or politics. Man
resents the loss of a rib, woman the rebuff from God,
those the beginning of a litany of slights that, piled end
on end, threatens to topple, inspiring one myth after another.
At last behaviour evolves into language, incident into
story, the stuttering "oh" of surprise into narrative. All
that remains is the ending, unexpected or pre-ordained,
who's to say, the shadow of the author's hand
fluttering like a bird.

Circus Vision

The eye of the owl sees in all directions
at once. It sees the death of the mouse,
sees its own death but doesn't blink. The eye
of the hawk is more focused, tunnel vision
in one exquisite gesture. It sees neither post
nor road yet knows its whereabouts
with precision and grace. The eye of the toad
is a circus, three rings at a time. It sees
the owl with one, the hawk with the other,
a collision course.

Religion

The sparrow's eye is on god.
And there is no end to the sparrow.
Her species are many and varied,
her thirst unquenchable. Look,
the trees are filled with sparrows
recreating the sounds of Babel,
filling the air with a species of joy.
In winter no less than in summer,
of sparrows there is no end. That thought
might be all the religion you need.

What Should We Do About Suffering?*

Suffering feels no compunction for us,
it has no conscience, no qualms or mercy.
It neither hesitates nor forgets, but stutters
in the face of hesitation, lisps in the shadow
of forgetting, in the soft white breath
of remembrance. Suffering, with its big belly,
breathes hot and moist into our ear,
against the nape of our neck, into the hollow
of our throat. Shameless, shameful, it has
designs on us, its own idea of the idea of us.
Suffering has no redeeming quality, no humour,
no grace. It knows well what to do about us,
but what should we do about suffering?

*a question posed in an essay by Anne Simpson

A Stopped Clock

The spiraling ball hovers in the plangent air.
It could go either way, straight to its true mark,
or as far wide as all the error we are capable of,
the weight of our hopes skewing its course.
Win or lose is beyond the point, each winner
harbouring a loss within, each loser right
at least once. *Tomorrow country*, they call it,
tomorrow and tomorrow and tomorrow,
all our tomorrows spiraling just out of reach,
the ball sinking at last to a confounding certainty.

Call and Response

I have heard the sweet mouth's siren call,
the sad sad song of the sour, the hopeful cry
rising from the beaks of blunted birds
bloody from the flesh of their prey.
How is it that beneath the feathered heart
lies the never-to-be-satisfied gut,
that the sallow loins of the lion ripple
for the thrill of the zebra's flight? Watching
the suicide of the sea turtle from the bow
of the Beagle, a tear came
to Darwin's eye, not for the turtle,
but for himself. Looking far
into the horizon he could see
his own extinction.

Stones

The afterlife of stone is air. From heaven,
intangible wisps float down to inspect
prints in sand where they once lay,
to wonder at the inexpressibleness
of their new existence. They whirl
in confusion, gently lifting grains of sand
in their wake. The grains coalesce,
fall to earth as stone, roll until they find
a familiar niche where they can be comfortable.
Ashes to ash, stones, of course, to stone.

Seasons

Summer is months gone but encores
in this bowl of raspberries in syrup,
so sweet, so red, right from the cellar jars,
seeds brittle in my teeth. Corn too, nuggets
of August, shivery beans and beets
in vinegar bath, honey in my tea
from summer's bees long after the hives
succumbed to snow. The seasons confound
us here, circling back upon themselves,
showing us a way to find our selves.

Descending

In the evening, when it cools, the old people
sit on the porch and watch the day take
its leave. If they sit very still, they too leave
their bodies and rise into the air the way
heat does. From the clouds they look
down, see their bodies sitting carefully
in Adirondacks and people passing by
on the sidewalk, voices rising gaily,
unaware. Heat, the light seeping out
of the day, those voices, the old people
themselves, all rising, as if evening
offers only a single direction until finally
there's an unspoken decision and, slowly,
with courtly grace, everything descends.

Three Songs of Dementia

1.
Long after you've forgotten my face, your mouth
remembers my name. I hear your lips whisper
its tender sound in the brief struggle of night.

2.
Despite myth and the best intentions of Hollywood,
Dracula grew old. He forgot his name – *dra, dra, la la la* –
the shape of his mother's throat, the comfort of the coffin.
His eyes filled with silver coins, his ears with moss
from the old country. Only his lips retained a rosy smear
of blood with its remembered scent.

3.
In time, all natural things forget.
Wood, fire, air fall away
with disinterest. Synthetics
remember their formula.
The song of wolves becomes echo
in the hollow night, musical notes
trembling with effort. The light
from distant stars travels on
through space and longing
long after their suns have exploded.

The River

1. Full of Itself

Where the river widens it is full of itself,
almost pompous, all dignified water, so deep
and still, practically a lake unto itself.
Where it narrows it grows jovial, tussling
for space with rocks and sweepers, offering
sprays of itself to the air for the gods
to inspect, burly water filled with froth
and fingernails. Along the sandy bars,
the river becomes humble, even obsequious,
turning its belly to you the way a puppy might,
bowing its head. Beneath the ragged cliffs
the river turns boastful again, daring itself to hurtle
faster and faster toward the roaring falls, but
as it goes over its knuckles blanche, its teeth
rattle, heart rocking against its ribs. At last,
in shallows, the river falls prayerful,
given to long soliloquies on the meaning
of its turbulent life. It hears the thrumming
of the sea in the distance and gathers
itself for the final plunge, the breaking out.

2. At Freeze-Up

The river moves too swiftly and nights
are not yet cold enough for ice
to harden, except in jagged bite marks
along its tender edges, forming a filigree
of primordial lace. Dazed, it races through
sluggish white landscape barely knowing
where it is, so changed is everything. Yet
the river itself is untouched, unshakeable,
a throbbing ribbon of mercury taking
the temperature of a stricken land.
A reverse fever sets in, leaving the patient
numb, delirious. The river holds
its own counsel against naysayers
and prognosticators, those who read the worst
into every shadow: six more weeks
of a frozen world. At night, it tumbles head
over heels, relentless, unrepentant.

3. Sees its Future

In January, the river finds itself weighed down
by ice encroaching from both banks, narrowing
its course. A slick of frozen froth rides
the darkened water's surface, blocking out
the sun. The river gasps for breath and thinks
of theology. Water has a dim memory
of hibernation, of diving deep beneath
a transformed version of itself to find
comfort in sleep. In its dreams, the river
hears mumbled words from a god promising
thaw, further transformation. It sees its future,
blindingly clear in its simplicity: water, ice,
fluid, solid, tears, salt, on and on through
the seasons, change the one constant. There is
a pleasing rhythm to this pattern, a solace
soothing fear. It is, the river comes to realize,
as simple as breathing itself.

4. Dreaming

The river fights off sleep. Just days ago, it was alive
to its icy surroundings, arrogant in its wanton run.
Now its waist cinched, its shoulders quilted
with downy comfort, it struggles to keep eyes open.
Soon, the river will dream its way to a new sea,
across the continental divide into uncharted waters,
waters free of fish and crustaceans, weed and reef,
any obstruction to the river's own muscular, musical
course. What bliss, to be free, finally able to find
its own level. Dreaming, the river sees itself
as it has never done before, a pure pulse
of forward motion, a propulsive narrative arc
leading to an uncertain ending. In its sleep,
the river rolls over, shivering with anticipation.

After the Death of the Dog

The polished oak beneath the table
where she curled pulses with light.
In the winter yard, a shallow bowl
of snow marks her absence, the birds
at the feeder sing as if she were there
to hear them, they don't mourn her
passing the way we do. They hear
her singing their way to the light.

Summer Solstice

The longest day of the year is weighted
with late summer heat. At noon the air is still,
saturated with its own juice. Then a high
keening among the leaves overhead,
trees hunching their shoulders, a moaning
of expectation – and a crack, as if heaven
itself has broken its vow of silence. The sky
pulls out all its stops, theatrical cloud chasing
its tail, ventriloquist wind, and the cottonwoods
begin to cough. Up north, so many words for snow,
but this feathery sugar is not one of them. The sky's
adrift with it, falling on your skin like a promise
or maybe a kiss. What's to come: a hush
and the revelations of afternoon, an evening
that will stretch on into a mere hiccup of night,
a bugger of a full moon. For now, content
yourself with this sweetness, this drowsy comfort.

Change and Departure

(for dee)

'To condense the diffused light of a page of thought into the luminous flash of a single sentence, is worthy to rank as a prize composition just by itself...Anybody can have ideas – the difficulty is to express them without squandering a quire of paper on an idea that ought to be reduced to one glittering paragraph.'
– Mark Twain

One glittering paragraph, that's all we're given
or allowed, all the weight the geese rehearsing
their departure overhead with proclamations
of joy and toil will bear. Change is coming,
the dry-leaves scent of it heavy on the wind
the geese stir up, the light diffused in their feathers
a prism through which a luminous flash of thought
radiates, carrying our hopes with them, south
then north again, cycles of time tattooed
on the webs of their feet. Change and departure,
distilled into that crystal moment.

Acknowledgments

Many of these poems appeared first, often in slightly different versions (and sometimes drastically different) in the following magazines: *Arc, Atlas, CV2, Canadian Literature, Crannog (Ireland), Descant, Existere, FreeFall, Humanist Perspective, Malahat Review, The New Quarterly, Queen's Quarterly, Poetry Review (England), Rattle* (U.S.), *The Society, untethered, Windsor Review*; and internet journals: *Fieldstone Review, Rusty Toque, SugarMule, Quint, Wascana Review, Your Daily Poem.* "*Descending*" was broadcast on *Sound Exchange*, CBC Saskatchewan.

In addition, "The day after" first appeared in *Crossing Lines: Poets Who Came to Canada in the Vietnam War Era*, Seraphim Editions, Niagara Falls, ON, 2008; and "My Father's Ghost" and "In the Days Before Summer's Arrival" in *Seek It: Writers and Artists Do Sleep*, Red Claw Press, Toronto, 2012.

My thanks to all the editors involved.

Thanks also to the welcoming and supportive staff and board of Coteau Books. And an enormous thanks to my brilliant editor, Maureen Scott Harris, who helped push these poems. I owe her a huge debt of gratitude.

– Dave Margoshes

About the Author

Dimensions of an Orchard, the last poetry collection by Dave Margoshes, won the Anne Szumigalski Poetry Prize at the 2010 Saskatchewan Book Awards. He's published four other books of poetry and over a dozen other books, including novels and short story collections. His poems have won a number of awards, including the inaugural Stephen Leacock Prize for Poetry, and have appeared widely in Canadian literary magazines and anthologies, including twice in the *Best Canadian Poetry* volumes. His *Bix's Trumpet and Other Stories* was 2007 Saskatchewan Book of the Year and a ReLit Award finalist. His collection of linked short stories, *A Book of Great Worth*, from Coteau, was named one of Amazon.Ca's Top Hundred Books of 2012. One of the stories from that collection was a finalist for the Journey Prize. He lives on a farm near Saskatoon.